WILD LIFE

MUSINGS OF A MAD POET

TY GARDNER

For more information address: gardnty@gmail.com

ISBN: 9798567887288

to all the mad poets
keep musing

Table of Contents

moon mood

i don't have anything to say today.

maybe tonight when the moon is in a mood.

state of the world

the world is in a state and the children are building sandcastles that i'd like to kick over and beat my chest in their faces. sometimes i just want to be a mongrel like that. some half human creature that skulks and pisses itself when beaten. wouldn't that be amusing? to get exactly what we want the moment we want it. toddlers have that you know? that authority to scream spittle mouthed demands without question. maybe that's all any of us want. to be angry when it counts. to kick and spit vitriol and piss ourselves every now and again. we're toddlers at the end of the day and the world is in a state. sagging like a fat breast engorged with polluted milk. i laugh a crows caw at the sight of chubby little fingers pinching and pawing at the mother's nipple.

skatepark teenagers

i should've known i'd be this way by now. the western sun on fall days drives the weirdos out in droves. drives me nuts to breathe their density. i'm not sure i've ever been happy. it's 80 degrees in the dead of winter and i can't say one good thing about it. i'm too focused on the idea that skatepark teenagers are careless and i couldn't dislike them more for that. they don't know anything about direction beyond where their wheels are pointed. but maybe that's the point i'm missing. nothing has to mean anything. point and push. lean and glide. repeat. dust yourself off after you eat concrete and keep moving. i guess i'd rather sit and stew about it. speak my piece in stanzas and covet from behind cheap sunglasses. pretty sure i've never been happy.

i'm bothered

i've been watching this homeless man for awhile. watching him watch the world and wondering what he's looking at. small humans argue stupidly behind me but i can't be bothered. chemtrails from winter inversion have settled in my lungs but still i can't be bothered. grown men are waxing their legs in a parlor somewhere but i can't be bothered. a virgin is giving herself to a man who will never love her. a father disowns his faggot kid. the sun rises and sets and the appeal of breasts and copulation have begun to mean nothing to me and again i can't be bothered. my apartment houses dust from decades of me not being bothered. bills and debt and death and dirt are all life will ever amount to but i really can't be bothered with that either. wealth. fame. love. lust. tight skin. good hair and health are just more things i can't be bothered with. there is only the homeless man standing and staring in an open field. he too cannot be bothered. and it bothers me to no end that i'm bothered by that.

not like it used to be

well it's friday night again. whatever that means. the violent thrum of the washing machine will be the only banging around here. what i wouldn't give to murder a bag of coke and rob a lemonade stand in the nouveau neighborhoods. walk around the back streets with a blindfold on and a pocket full of pennies and see who could use some change in their lives. it'll be saturday morning soon. not like it used to be though. peanut buttered pancakes and pissing the dog. dad sure knew how to turn a phrase and mom was quick with the coffee. real people. nothing special. there's probably more to it but the mind recalls what it wants. i guess that's all i prefer to remember. pancakes and pissing the dog. not the other stuff. anyways sounds like the washing shut off. better go change the laundry over. it'll be saturday morning soon. not like it used to be.

don't ask me to iron

don't ask me to iron anything today. it's cloudy outside and i'd rather watch the brewer sparrows dive bomb into my bedroom window. cretinous little mutants. i've never seen a creature reproduce with such meaningless greed. humping then carrying and hatching and chirping relentlessly to be fed then growing up and repeating their parent's life cycle before dive bombing into my window. i desperately want them to break their necks to relieve them of their pointless existence. or maybe i'm just projecting. perhaps i'll dream myself a sparrow humping and feeding and dive bombing into someone's window. it won't even occur to me to use my gift of flight to do something with purpose. no i'll want to be just like my parents before me. breeding stupidly into someone's backside before finally figuring out that none of it means anything. hoping to god that the next dive bomb will break my neck. someone please ask me to iron something today.

bury me with a smile

i'd like to be more like the sloth on my bed. a cushy thing with a pleasant smile stitched to its face. he sits there just so without a care in the world. even when we put him in the microwave and roast him on high to warm us on cold days he sits there just so. when we fart and snore and breathe sex breath in the still of night he sits there just so with a pleasant smile stitched to his face. i like to think he's trying to tell me something but i know i'll never get it. my mouth isn't fixed and i care about all the things i shouldn't. time is tricky that way and that's the thing my cushy friend will never understand. someday when the time comes i'll ring up the mortician and tell him i don't care anymore. i'll ask him to stitch me up a smile like my cushy sloth and that'll be the end of it. they'll bury me with that smile and my sloth will go on sitting without a care in the world knowing something i never did.

things that don't want to be forgotten

seems like there's some things i'll just never shake. recollections that can't be burned out of my brain ya know? believe me i've tried. tried to scrub them away with alcohol. to pepper them with drugs. season them a bit and change the flavor. tried to throw some gray in and dull the color but the childhood image of my younger brother and i burying our murdered puppy on a bitter cold winter afternoon isn't the kind of thing that cooks out. standing over a hole and a hefty bag with a dead dog inside doesn't wash off so easy and holding hands with a weeping child in the dull burnout of a chalky haze is hauntingly vibrant despite the careful strokes. i go back there sometimes. i know the way. i shouldn't but i do. i've found that some things don't want to be forgotten and i think that maybe i get a sort of peace from feeding that memory. feeding that dead dog. my brother lives far away now in a different small town. i think that he prefers to keep himself haunted.

the courtyard tree

there's a tree in the courtyard below my balcony that looks sick. i'm wondering about asking if it's okay. i'm reminded of a cancer patient in chemotherapy. the sparse leaves are dangling noncommittally like desperate strands of hair that can't decide whether to brave the fall or hang on awhile longer. the tree looks skeletal. not like i remember and i think i will walk down and ask if it's okay. but anything unimportant has just distracted me and so i think i may go down tomorrow instead.

plain walls

plain walls really displease me. i can feel their judgment like they're so much better than everyone else. stupid plain walls with their thoughtfully placed textures and carefully sanded surfaces. i'd be perfect too if god thought to put in any effort. i guess i should be more grateful. i'm covered with moles and cracks and craters. character i think they call it. either way we're both unpleasant to look at. they're judgy and i'm spoiled by character. aren't we a pair? plain walls and me? somehow i know that's not the kind of comparison anyone will ever make. people don't care to think harder than they have too. must be why i don't care for them either. they're boring and judgy and i'm spoiled by character.

privilege and fixtures

it's a hell of a thing walking out your front door wondering if today's the day they pull your sorry carcass off the sidewalk. blood and brain matter sinew spread out like jellied toast. terrified mothers pulling desperately at curious children who can't take their eyes off of the last thing i'll ever be to anyone and texting their husbands to tell them that they love them knowing good and well that they really don't. it's been a good 10 years but privilege and posh neighborhoods and fancy fixtures have driven them apart and into the arms of bored and boring lovers who dislike their own spouses and privilege. and then those mothers will try to figure out when and where everything got so bungled up? on the way home they'll stop at a drive thru and stare absently at the menu before they tell the gum chewing teen on the other end that they'll just have a couple of orders of fried convenience please. for the remainder of the drive they'll tune out their garbage disposals in the backseat and reflect their dismal humanity. perhaps tonight they'll make love to their spouse. maybe even allow for some light petting. it's been a while right? long enough anyway. and in the morning they'll call their life insurance agent and take them up on that offer to shift their policies into high risk after all. the markets been doing well lately and something has to pay for fancy fixtures and privilege if they bite the dust sooner than later. before putting the kiddos to bed they'll be feeling particularly vulnerable and want to do a phone call with grandpa over at the nursing home. not too long though something droll and pointless will be on the t.v. to help pass the time before the grand performance of scripted moaning and orchestrated orgasms begin. they'll want to wrap that up tout suite and get to bed quickly. a couple of the gals down the street are power walking bright and early and they've been dying to model those expensive leggings that cover belly fat and hike up sagging back ends. meanwhile i'm being pieced together on a slab of cold steel back at the morgue. and so it goes. some of us will wind up sidewalk glitter. the rest of us will go on living for high risk bonds and fancy fixtures.

incontinent dogs

there's an ignorance in this one horse town that makes my beard hurt. i don't even want to talk about it but i suppose i have to. i'm standing in the city park right? minding my own business when the trumpeting of a great walrus haul out comes parading down main street. honest to god real humans in their lifted pickup trucks with confederate flags adorned with the president's face on them. a whole train of them dancing to country whoop while drunk on crap beer and sneering their opinion all over the pavement like incontinent dogs. like i said it hurts my beard to think of humanity as jeering pigs advocating for idiocracy but there i was minding my own business when the trumpeting pollution train made its way down main street farting diesel fumes. i had to crawl into a dark hole and lick my liberal wounds when the little white kids told the hispanic kids that they couldn't wait until the wall was finished.

desert towns are weird

must've been about 10 the first time i saw a prostitute. i don't know that there's much to say about it. the night was salty with bakersfield summer air. or maybe that was just my aunt's temperament funking up the front seat. well anyway my cousin whooped like this one time when i was at the zoo and i pointed at an ape's breasts and made a big deal of it to the other kids. my mother damn near beat me to death right then and there. my aunt had that same look on her face that night. i don't recall much about the prostitute but i've never forgotten the way disappointed mothers look at their sons. desert towns are weird man.

christmas '95

christmas morning. '95. they came to tell us you'd killed yourself. pulled mom into the kitchen to have a sit down about the whole ordeal. brother and i had just unwrapped a landslide of gifts which i find humbling now. we were dirt poor back then. damn good haul that morning. hell of a christmas. slept like a baby that night dreaming of all those new goodies. slept right through mother's sobbing. at the viewing i could only stare at a bizarre version of you lying peacefully in your casket. christmas goodies were waiting at home to be played with. what did i know about death after all? mother told me years later about how quiet i'd been about everything. something about being reflective at such a young age. made me sound like some kind of old soul. i think though that i was just bitter about you ruining christmas. i'd even had a thought to ask if i could have your video game consoles. what did i know about death after all? i thought better of it in the end but now you know. that's the honest truth and i'll always hate myself for caring more about christmas goodies than the fact that you were gone for good. what did i know about death after all? 40's creeping up on me now and i'm thinking about two and a half decades since you died. there'll be no goodie landslide for my kids. a few simple things here and there. nothing to write about. you're the ghost of christmas past these days saving me from my selfishness and i'm better for it. i guess i did learn a thing or two from death after all.

parks and people

saturday. 2:30 and it's raining. slapping down like god's shaking one out. i'm watching this woman load her groceries in a vehicle that isn't worth the payment. i hate the shape of it. hate her bohemian style. hate the way she's loading her groceries in the downpour. she's trying too hard not to care about anything and it's obvious. there's a park just in front of me. unkempt and forgotten. ugly like the bohemian woman. both wear their contempt out on their face. how do parks and people get that way i wonder. careless and contemptible. is this what happens when we don't cherish each other? i won't see that woman ever again but the park will remember her. they live here and i don't. the sun comes out for a moment to say something. probably to someone else i guess and then it's gone again.

musings of a mad poet

i just passed myself going in the opposite direction. it happens from time to time but i don't mind it. i never notice myself when it happens but i always notice me when it does. sounds like the musings of a mad poet when i say it like that. it's been a wild life i suppose and i hope that the end isn't too far off. i've got the daddy bones now and there's a few graves i've yet to dance on before i go. maybe that's where other me was headed just now. must have had the same idea. i might be caught up on my grave dancing after all. probably not though knowing that idiot. i really don't like that guy. i'll probably give myself the finger when i see me again. and i'll probably finger me back. we'll both write about it and publish it in a book knowing us.

putting off the grocer

suppose i need to make a run to the grocer but the stench of stale pumpkins rotting in the hall makes me anxious. smells like a memory i have of working as a ranch hand for a child molester. i don't recall how we all wound up in his basement but i've never forgotten the terrifying tingle of his finger tickling the length of my spine. we went up as a group to the garage to have a smoke and i made sure never to be alone with him after that day. the two things aren't related but that's not the point. weird smells make me anxious and reflective and people should be throwing out their rotten pumpkins. so now i have to go have a long talk about the dangers of neglectful consumerism on my mental well being with my neighbor instead of going to the grocer. the whole day is shot and the neighbors probably aren't home anyway.

the writing on the bath wall

today's snow smacks of hunter thompson's suicide. the kind of snow that sounds like a cocked gun over the telephone. i don't know why i see life that way but i agree with the man's philosophy. i'm 17 more than i wanted. i might have more to say about that but i've just taken an interest in an ink smudge i'd forgotten about entirely. i'd scribbled something on the bath wall but didn't care for it. i remember pushing my finger across it and thinking how curious it was that something i'd written didn't die when i smudged it. on the contrary. it went on to live as a black stain forever imprinted on my bath wall. i think hunter understood that about words.

we don't talk about things

somewhere on a stretch of dead end just outside of evanston wyoming i sat in the backseat of my parent's bronco truck staring out the window at miles of sage and dust. just below the highway an old dirt road ran alongside and i noticed a small white sedan keeping pace with us. i thought that was interesting as we were traveling at highway speeds and the dirt road below looked washed and weather worn. and yet the sedan kept the pace. the driver of the car below realized all too late that the dirt road made an abrupt turn to the left and through an underpass beneath the highway. i watched as the little sedan sailed off into the unknown but lost sight of it as our road too began to curve. i'd seen the approaching bend and thought to shout and pound the window to get the driver's attention but the end result would still have been the same. i think my father would have been mad about the window anyway. we never spoke about the sedan save for those few seconds after the incident. what was there to say? i don't think they wanted to be put out when i look back on it. they'd lived long enough to know that about themselves. i realize now that my father was quieter than usual for the rest of that trip. maybe he does think more about things than i think he does. but i'll never know. we don't talk about things.

i am not the same

fruit flies have gathered in the meat section of the market downtown and somewhere in the back alleys of bad memories there's a deer carcass stuffed into the trunk of a 90s oldsmobile. i'm standing there with my stepfather on the shoulder of a one lane road in the middle of nowhere as he adjusts the legs to fit in the already cramped space. there's blood everywhere and the deer's eyes seem to follow me as i shift uneasily back and forth. it's true what they say about deer tongues hanging stupidly out of the side of their mouths in death. i think that part makes me the most uneasy. it's the innocence of it. the questioning stupidity that gives me the creeps. well the sun's setting and i've killed this thing close enough to a farmhouse that my stepfather suggests that we get moving before it gets too dark or the cops show up. whichever comes first. we make it to my father's house and pop the trunk for him to have a look. he gives an affirming nod and goes back to his beer. my stepfather and i drive back home in the dark but i am not the same.

something boozenly poetic

i never would have believed that the most alive i'd ever feel is in the steadying of a loaded gun against my head. that there's a liberating chaos in that space between certainty and uncertainty. life as you currently know it and the part that comes next. i never would have believed that a person could feel so empowered and so incredibly terrified at the same time. i chased that high for years but would not know those feelings again until i held my son for the first time. these may be the ramblings of a 4 a.m. drunkard but there has to be some sense in that correlation. maybe it's that we have to live long enough to understand that taking a life and giving one is an equally empowering and incredibly terrifying feeling. that there's certainty in the uncertain and vice versa and that the things we would never think to believe can change us in deeply affecting ways can. or something boozenly poetic like that.

the comfort of darkness

it's past my bedtime again. sometime around 10:30 and i'm wide awake listening to the darkness. it's telling me about this night when i was 15. blackout drunk in the back of a broken down pickup truck stored at the rear of a trailer park. i'd come to after a few too many gins and raised hell about my missing cigarette to the others sitting around me. they just laugh wildly and it all comes back that i'd stubbed the stupid thing out in my palm on a dare. the darkness goes on to tell me how lucky i am to have its friendship. that it would never laugh at me like that or dare me to do something as reckless as stubbing out a cigarette in my palm. it asks only for my deepest thoughts and darkest fears as payment to keep me company. i am comforted by the darkness.

life at a stop sign

there's life happening at a stop sign. funny to think about. seconds ticking away. fingers tapping on the steering wheel. the radio plays a song about being afraid of changing and how time makes you bolder. boy that takes me back. high school happens all over again in my head and i'm coming over the hill late one night with my buddy in that old hooptie escort and suddenly there's police sirens everywhere. turns out an upperclassman we know's just been killed in a motorcycle accident. my buddy and i don't know what to say and drive on listening to songs that meant something to us then but lose value over time. graduation isn't far off for the rest of the seniors that year and that's a heavy thought for a couple of guys our age. the car behind honks me back into reality and the song on the radio comes to an end.

makes me wonder

windy days irritate me. i always wonder about this abandoned trailer where this kid's mom that i went to school with was killed. i think about this one time he smarted off to me and i jokingly asked him if he kisses his mother with that mouth. we stare stupidly at each other and i should have apologized but honestly i was too embarrassed. we stayed friends to a certain point up until i finished school and moved out of town. he was only good to me for drugs and a laugh. he later threatened to kill me over a girl he'd dated and abused and he wasn't good to me for anything after that. he wasn't good for anything or anybody to be flat honest and i didn't think much about it when he overdosed on drugs and died years later. so on windy days i think about the whistling sounds that blow through and haunt that abandoned trailer where his mother was killed. i guess i should have apologized for what i said about her when we were kids. makes me wonder how different he'd have been with a better start to life. when the wind dies down i'll think about something else.

the worth of my salt

scars are my new curiosity lately. i can pick out each one individually and know its meaning right away. the one on my left shoulder for example where an old metal hanger with the end bent into a circle was left over a campfire until it got white hot and then pressed into my skin. a symbol of good times with friends i haven't spoken to in over 20 years branded onto my arm to carry with me until my death so that i'll never forget. but i forget whatever it was that i wasn't supposed to. i only recall the white hot end of that metal hanger pressing into my skin. i didn't scream. what good would that have done? how else could i have proved my salt's worth otherwise? well that wound festered and fussed for weeks after that and i thought i might lose my arm a couple of times but at least i had my salt. i like that about myself now. not the part about the salt but that i don't have anything to prove.

10 years and change

a little over 10 years and some change i found my way back to my granddad's gravesite. the teton mountain range in the distance had a demeanor about it. i don't know. you'd have had to be there i guess. i think it might have been angry with me for not coming around sooner. for not showing up after granddad's stroke and before he passed away. for the way his children gazed emptily at his remains before he went into the ground for good. for no one else showing up in that whole 10 years to say hello. could have been any one of those things i guess. i just know that i need to go back again before another 10 years and some change. i don't like the tetons being mad at me.

like i was taught

it was me or the marmot. we'll start with that. the barrel end of the family's 45 revolver pooted smoke and burnt gunpowder but i held my stance like i was taught. feet shoulder width apart. isosceles style. i kept my eye trained right down the site and on the creature at the other end. the bullet had hit square on. smack in the guts. the little bugger writhed and flopped for a moment but finally conceded its death. i holstered up and sauntered on over to stand above my kill. ground squirrel. clean shot. i think i spit or maybe even shined my boot for effect. i was a big man that day. like i said it was me or the marmot. just like i was taught.

on death and dying

got thinking the other day about death and dying. what it means to me and whether i'm afraid of it. do i have any regrets? that sort of thing. well i've held the hands of dying men who were tougher than anyone i know and there's just no two ways about it. when they burst into tears you do too. when they tell you through coughing fits of crying how they wish they'd said and done more you know at that moment what they're really getting at. what you should be doing differently. so am i afraid of death and dying? no. i'm okay with the things i can't control. i'm terrified of not being remembered. of not doing enough to sustain my legacy. if you're reading this i'm a part of you now and you'll know i have no regrets.

must be something

headaches again. must be the city sidewalks and red lights. the target moms and their bougie toddlers. the divisiveness of social media and the stupidity of arguing the safety of vaping pens vs. cigarettes. must be the honking horns in rush hour traffic and the polarization of politics. must be all the talk of god and trying to debunk the theory of evolution. must be the climate change and piggishness of people. the curiosity of animal lovers who enjoy a good steak. must be the coffee snobs who prefer to pay $10 for a small cup and the people who still use checks at the grocery store. must be the governor telling my kids they can go to school during a pandemic but not to the playground. must be the hypocrisy in teaching our children not to take candy from strangers unless it's halloween. must be the way some people make right hand turns and online newspapers asking me to pay for a subscription. must be the people with big families complaining about overpopulation again. all i know is that the headaches are back so it must be something.

if it ain't broke

wet rice on the kitchen floor wants to pick a fight with me. knows good and well that if i try to sweep it up right now it will stick and smear across the linoleum. we both know my mental state can't handle that so i decide to walk away for the time being. maybe go file my taxes or wait in line at the post office. anything to take my mind off wet rice and sticky kitchen floors. the trick is to find something so banal and pointless and soul crushing and utterly unimportant to human existence to distract me so that when i come back the rice will be dried and easy to sweep up. sometimes i just need to trade up one stupid thing for another to feel better. i don't question the philosophy. if it ain't broke etc. etc.

how to be an adult

latchkey kids don't mind a lot of things. that sticks out to me after all these years. i can't even count how many times we spit in each other's faces and chucked rocks at one another and ran around the house with kitchen knives in a blind rage. we didn't make anything of it just kept coming and going. put the key in the lock. turn quarter clockwise. come and go. back. forth. spit. chuck. chase. repeat. make the meal and fold the clothes. finish the chores. key in the lock. coming and going. quarter clockwise turn. come and go. spit. eat. chuck. fold. finish. repeat. i learned a lot about being an adult from being a latchkey kid. the grown ups in my house were doing the same thing just with a driver's license. coming. going. spitting. chucking. chasing and eating. but we never did mind. we learned how to be adults from being latchkey kids. and that sticks out to me after all these years.

vegas after divorce

las vegas has its own frequency after divorce. a mood that hangs over the city like a shawl. i like to be there right in the thick of things. just after the papers are signed but before the ink dries. it's a great place to shake out the dust and demons and fall in love for the night. strippers are best for that i find. they're more sincere with their time and willingness to listen. i think maybe they've had it harder than most. i like to treat them well and show them compassion before i leave again. it gives me a sense of peace on the lonely drive back home. that stretch of desert always makes me think too much. there's just nothing else you can do out there. i wonder about my ex and what i could have done differently. about the strippers and if they're happier now having met me. if i made an impact in their life somehow. i wonder if they maybe even loved me back just a little. i think i prefer to think about things that way after vegas. the lonely desert has its own frequency after all. A shrill frequency of ex wives and negative bank accounts and i don't care to think about those things.

gray hairs and cracks

checking for gray hairs has become cathartic and i'm getting comfortable with the cracks in my face. i like the reminders of the little things. the crash and burn of first kisses. the violence in young relationships and how the stars look in moonless canyons going 120 in a car that can't handle the curves. the burying of best friends before their 18th birthday and visiting your parents behind bars. the thrill of running from the cops and the camaraderie found when they finally catch you. the sting of a slapped cheek from talking back and the sinking feeling of giving one to someone else. a gray hair and crack line for all the things i can count and the ones i can't. for every pill i have to take to correct a thing i did back when. a gray hair and crack. and i don't mind that.

sad songs need to feel loved

can you truly blame a sad song for putting you down in the dumps? i mean really hurting your feelings with every single line like it's picking on you just to make itself feel better? i like to think myself rather unselfish that way. i prefer to listen to a sad song over and over and let it abuse my emotions. i'm tough like that. sad songs have to live that way forever but i can change my tone when i pick and choose. i can match my mood to any melody i please whenever i see fit. sad songs just want to be loved like the rest of us i think. so what's a couple of hours being in a funk to help a sad song feel better?

2 a.m.

2 a.m. seems like

a good time to

ask myself what

it's all about.

memories of a horse

thoughts of life in a small town come to me in black and white these days. it might have something to do with this horse we kept behind our house. i don't remember anything about it specifically. i never rode it or had anything to do with it except for filling up five gallon buckets with water to keep it hydrated. that might be the part i'm bitter about. caring for something i didn't have a care for. i'm not even sure what happened to that horse but i haven't forgotten the buckets of water and caring for things i don't have a care for. that part never left me. i'm still carrying the water and caring for things i don't care for. someday someone will carry my water and care for me. i just can't be sure that they'll care for me or if i'll just be their black and white memory of a horse.

headlights at dark

headlights at dark put me in a place. everything around me falls off and i'm 18 again down a deserted road in a winding canyon with nothing but my bad attitude and shadowed things fleeing from the moon. i'm parked in the dirt and dry grass watching my cell phone light up again and again but i'm not taking her calls right now. i've got other things on my mind and i don't want her talking me out of it. suddenly there's a spotlight in my window blinding me. blue and red flash and bounce off the canyon walls and then there's a man tapping the glass on my door. the man asks me for my license and registration and what i'm doing out this far by myself at this time of night. i'm quick on my feet and make up something satisfactory. i don't want him talking me out of it either. he seems content with my story and tells me it's time to pack it up and move along. so i do. his headlights keep a reasonable distance as he follows me back into town before he splits off and i'm alone again. part of me thinks to drive on and find a new place to park and start over but i'm tired now and a warm bed sounds better at this point. it dawns on me years later that i never saw the man's face and i wonder about god. if god is just a faceless stranger that shows up on deserted roads at night. if it's just coincidence or if there's any meaning to it. headlights at dark put me in that place.

the sum of it

a thought occurred to me recently that i've not recalled for some time of a hot summer day and a magnifying glass. i'd gathered a mess of grasshoppers and shoved them into a large bottle. my brother begged me not to do it but the temptation for chaos was overwhelming and i'd concentrated a sunbeam through the magnifying glass onto the body of one of the more buried insects in the bottle until it began to smolder and eventually took flame. one by one the legged leapers joined their friends popping from heat and combustion. it didn't occur to me that creatures that small could scream but i know it now as surely as anything i'm certain of. again my brother pleaded and tried to stop the madness. i ended up kicking him so hard for it that our father had to carry him back inside the house. the rest of the day was hot and uneventful which sums up that entire summer. and i think it also sums up parts of my life and why i am the way i am. times were hot and uneventful and that sums it up.

people are peculiar

something about that last bend coming around the lake on the way to grandmother's house just gets people. truckers mostly. they always end up on their side. twisted metal and glass everywhere. mostly i mind my business and drive by without much regard. other times though the cargo is livestock or whatever's left of it after the truck slides to a stop. people get peculiar when there's blood involved. brings out their baser instincts and suddenly there's a line to see the show. the policeman stands like a circus leader ushering people through and honking his big rubber nose while waving his tophat to the crowd in the back. i'm more interested in the policeman and the circus goers. that's the real show for me. people are peculiar when there's blood involved.

letter to a younger me

all right you with the rebel flag wallet and nazi swastikas taped to your bedroom window. you with the sleeveless shirt and cigarette dangling from your lips. with the bad attitude towards women and people of color. the one poking fun at the man who lives by a bench downtown. you who are so many things right now that you won't be. you're not ready for the brown wife who will give you mixed babies. you're not ready for compassion in understanding how people come to be crippled by the world. you're not ready for words that will change lives and inspire truth. so for now i'll just pack this letter up for later along with the others. and somewhere an older me is packing his letters for another time too. a time when i'm ready just as you will be someday.

these are one night stands

i drifted off in the tub again dreaming about a one night stand. whiskey wasted and panting like an idiot. there's nothing special about the dream. it's dark and i can't see a thing. i like it better that way. lets me keep my dignity. the lights come on without warning and i quickly realize there's no one there but me. naked and alone. i come to in the tub and the water's gone frigid. this is what one night stands feel like. naked. cold and alone.

houses i used to live in

sort of strange about houses i used to live in. they seem lonelier than i remember whenever i drive by. the paint faded and duller and the shutters cracked from weather wear. one day i may knock and ask to visit the walls inside and see if they still know me. but i suppose they probably won't so why bother? i'm not the me i was and they probably have a few coats of paint since i last saw them. i do that with people too it seems. but i don't find that strange. people are transient. they'll find each other if they choose to. not like houses i used to live in. they're always right there where i left them until they're not. and i find that sort of strange.

we are our parents

tugging at my ear for the thousandth time today. seems like i'm just waiting for the tinnitus to kick in. there's a high pitch deep in the canal that tickles my tongue in a painful way. like how i got screamed at as a kid. i try to push my fingertip into my eardrum to block the noise but the pitch is already inside and i can only tug again. i scream at my own kids now. not because they did anything wrong. i just want to drown out that pitch. i remember the past and i'm doomed to repeat it. we are our parents. screaming and tugging at our ears. pushing our fingers into the tinnitus.

minecart memory

maybe if i rub my eyes a little harder i'll brush out the tired. seems reasonable so i push a little harder until that burnt film strip effect takes over and there's a still of this man on the venice beach pier pleading with me to accept god into my heart in order to save my soul. i hate that memory so i push harder. the next still is heat bubbled even worse but i still recognize the little playground in the trailer park i grew up in. i'm sitting in a minecart that seems out of place but is there all the same. one of the neighbor kids has defecated in the cart and still i remain. i don't know why i sat in the cart like that but i'm more tired from dredging up childhood memories and now my eyes hurt.

nighttime at the nursing home

nighttime at the nursing home where i did my time as a nurse's assistant still gives me a feeling of foreboding. i learned a great deal about death roaming the halls in the small hours. standing in darkened doorways listening to residents pleading to die while sitting at the edge of their beds with their heads in their hands. that struck me deeply that a person could beg desperately for something so infinite. but time and circumstance have given me clarity and i no longer question that pleading desperation. i do however feel the heat of death's breath on my neck from time to time in thoughts of nighttime at the nursing home. i feel that heat and i write. i write until my hand hurts and my head is empty. i hope to write all the things before i too am alone with my head in my hands and my thoughts at night in the nursing home.

something random

something random. like the time i snagged a brown trout with a treble hook. gave a hard yank and caught it right in the guts. reeled it in and watched it flop about on the grassy shore. hollered and pounded my fist in the air as the poor thing's eyes bulged out of its head gasping for breath. life got me like that as i grew older. snagged in the guts with a treble hook gasping for breath on the grassy shore. i am a brown trout. something random.

harriet

harriet. perfectly fitting name for the ugliest mutt you've ever laid your eyes on. we loved her from minute one though. can't recall the breed. small dog with black fur and a graying snout. hand to god that dog was indestructible. as old as she was she could chase a car with the best of them. every day she was at it. running her arthritic legs off barking like she had rabies or something. not sure what she had to prove but she was persistent. the number of times she got hit by passing cars and kept going left us speechless. and when she took a rear tire to the face on one occasion and had her nose broken and scraped almost clean off she didn't flinch. even when she tangled herself up with a stray male and i tried to beat them both with a stick to make them separate she just kept at it. did things her way till the bitter end and now i understand why. life's a crooked nose mutt that does what it wants and we're just cars passing through.

falling out of moving cars

falling out of moving cars puts things in perspective. even at 5 years old it's the kind of thing that leaves a lasting impression on a person. the way you roll across moving traffic praying to god that you don't wind up as someone's hood ornament can really make you wonder about divine intervention as you age. you might ask yourself why the universe would spare your life. ask if you're meant for something more and that's why that pickup truck swerved just in time. puts quite a load on a 5 year old. puts quite a load on the guy wondering if 30 years later he's living up to the legacy put before him. or if any of it means anything. maybe the driver of the pickup was just particularly attentive. perhaps there are questions that are better unanswered. like would i be this way now if i hadn't fallen out of a moving car at 5 years old? some questions probably are better left unanswered.

all the could've

i could've dressed better for the funerals of friends i've buried. could've said a kind word when it counted. i could've stayed a little longer. could've laughed more and cried less. i could've leapt. could've looked first. could've been there. could've done that. could've asked first. could've shot later. i could've fought less. could've fought more. i could've said something. could've kept quiet. i could've lied when it came up. could've told the truth when it didn't. i could've worked harder. could've taken more time. i could've gave a hug. could've held a hand. i could've said no more. could've said yes less. i could've made a list of all the things i could've done. probably could've done them all by now.

everclear margarita

it was about that 3rd everclear margarita

that i realized i'd made a terrible mistake.

miles between us

drove it till it broke down on the highway in the middle of nowhere. that little red metro a girlfriend bought for nothing. the three of us took one last look at it before hopping a barbed wire fence and disappearing into the darkness. open fields lie before us. two feet of snow over a frozen landscape of hidden creeks to cross to notch up the good times. no clue where we were going but we knew we had to put miles between us and that metro. into the night we ran. stumbled and splashed and soaked ourselves to the bone. but still we ran. decades have come and gone and that old metro is long abandoned to rust and overgrowth. and still we run trying to put miles between us.

for a few quick dollars

the sounds of hard braking brought me out of whatever dream state i was in at the time and i jumped up in my seat to see what the commotion was about. my father had stopped short at the site of a rusted vehicle decaying in the midday sun in an empty field. i don't recall him ever being so animated over anything. the excitement in his voice as he explained what lay before us was highly unusual and i'd made a mental note of it to pour over and analyze later. by complete and random circumstance we'd happened upon an old ford mustang that he'd owned as a younger man. he told my brother and me how he'd been restoring the machine but had needed to sell it for a few quick dollars. we watched as he ran his hands over sanding marks on the hood that were decades old. the same marks made by much younger hands. the air was dense and quiet as he removed the emblem from the vehicles interior. an emblem that sits on his mantel still. an emblem that will sit on my own mantel someday. something i can run my finger over from time to time. a symbol of the only memory that made any sense of who my father was.

the way i yell

the way i yell sometimes is
deeply rooted in memories
of repaired drywall.

even when the sun is out

i'm watching my parents cry and hug as my father puts the last of his belongings in that old beater of his. the sun is out so i'm not sure why i'm circling back around to that again. memories are cyclical like that. i'm older in the vision sitting with my younger self explaining that this is just how things go with moms and dads. course he doesn't understand. naturally. i tell him it will make more sense in time when he's older. tell him that in a year or two from now he'll be lying in bed with our father listening to him weep over our mother and it will start there. that he'll be hard on our mother for many years because of it but that people change and so does the way they prioritize others. that one day he'll be sitting with a younger version of us having this same conversation because memories are cyclical that way even when the sun is out.

too cool for god

i can't say i'll ever believe in god. i know god's reached out to me plenty of times. tried to talk to me but i've always been too cool to talk back. i never wanted to acknowledge that mysterious tapping on my shoulder that time i was alone with my thoughts. or the way that patch of black ice didn't send me spinning into a frozen lake one night when i swerved to avoid hitting a deer. i certainly had nothing to say when i suddenly had second thoughts and decided not to pull that trigger. yessir i've always fancied myself too cool to talk to god. chalk it all up to coincidence i suppose. maybe one day when all my adventures are coming to an end and i'm clean out of coincidences i won't be too cool. when the terrors of wondering what comes next keep me up at night maybe then i won't be too cool.

that one night

that one night when we were stupid and stoned and heckling passing cars for the hell of it. that one night when the e tards were skin to skin in group love ecstasy. that one night when we were punching each other's faces to prove something. that one night campfire kissing a girl that wasn't mine. that one night trying to keep it between the highway lanes. that one night putting it all on red and pissing away the mortgage. that one night outrunning the cops because of boredom. that one night when we were broke down in the mountains. that one night when we laughed and had it all. that one night before the last night. the last time we would have your all.

discarded carnys

discarded cigarettes in sidewalk cracks are like the carny kids i would run with. people walk past or over top of them without a second glance but if you light one up they'll show you a good time at no charge.

video game apocalypse

delivery truck kid is sitting in the front seat of his rig biting his fingernails and spitting skin flakes and grease all over the steering wheel. and it hits me that this reckless maniac is about to cause the apocalypse. some other nail biting fool will drive that truck next week and he'll go to chew his fingers and suck in that other kid's germs and suddenly he's come down with whatever that kid has and then he'll eventually cough into his old lady's face but she won't think much of it and the next thing you know she's smooching her lover while her nail biter is at work and then that person comes into contact with his people and soon enough those numbers double and then those numbers double and without warning there's a water and toilet paper shortage and nobody dares go to the grocery store. people are dropping like flies and we implement a face mask mandate but it's already too late. zombies start cropping up and the world is a hit television show. all because some nail biting nimrod spit his bad habit all over the steering wheel of his company truck. now sure i may have gone down a rabbit hole on this one but that's where my mind goes when my kids start talking to me about their video games.

a day of reflection

today's a day of wind and snow. smells like wrecked childhood out there. smells like age and gray inside. today is a day of reflection.

speaking for my people

in the end whiskey and ash will be the pulpit stories of my people. they'll have lived hard and sinned but i will speak and lie for them.

leaving my regrets in ink

i've got regrets same as anyone else. high school romances and drug encounters. cheating and alcohol abuse. running with the devil in the desert moonlight. tattoos and fistfights and hate for folks i don't know. lied and stole from good people and laughed about it. watched things burn and skipped out on funerals of friends. yeah i've got regrets same as anyone else. and i'm leaving them here in ink because i don't need them anymore. never did me any good to keep and carry them around. so i'm leaving them here in ink.

waiting for grandpa

september and the winds are out. it's my wedding anniversary but i'm sitting at the grand's house waiting for grandpa to pass. we've said our piece and made him comfortable. i'm in the next room laughing at a television show and he's in there taking his last breaths. but we've said our piece and made him comfortable. he doesn't want us in there. wants to do the dying his way. i admire him for that. well 6 a.m. rolls around and he lets go for good as we stand around with wet eyes. the rain pounds the tin roof outside and it feels like a million years have passed since i was in the other room laughing. the rain keeps on pounding outside but we've said our piece.

freckles and moles

tried a therapist once. couldn't get into it. everything was supposed to be someone else's fault for the way i turned out. somebody somewhere did something that i never let go of and now i'm sitting on an over expensive couch talking it out with some guy who's just as bored as i am about the whole thing. i think the only thing i got for my money was a pricey outlet to designate blame. but something about that didn't sit right so i decided to stop paying for something i'd already been doing all along. putting my problems on bad marriages between people who did the same to those before them and so on. drinking and drugging things down the way i was taught to round off the hard edges of a bad day. because a leopard can't change its spots. we are who we are as they say. but something about that didn't sit right either. in the end i realized we're freckles and moles. some of it is just in the genes. the rest of it is a cluster of our craziness that builds into hard bumps. they might look the same but there's a difference. and we can choose which one we want to be. something about that sits right.

cherry angioma poetry

cherry angiomas are cropping up all over. bones pop and threaten to break when i bend over and white wine weekends always end with crusted kidneys. bartop dancing and hanging out taxi windows losing my lunch on the rolling pavement came and went with kids. passing the pipe and tucking 20s in stringed undies or the sunrise on mountaintops and random road trips are just things i write about now. anything that meant something is just bad skin and creaky joints these days. little cherry angiomas cropping up all over that i write about now.

syl

we're all a little syl some days. 30 slaps like an open hand. i've felt it. and death is the only thing we care to write about. there's nothing exotic about life after 30. anything interesting happens before 25. just before that internal clock goes off and the pressure to put on your adult skin sets in. well you put on the skin and do the things. buy the house. punch the clock. have the kids. punch the clock. pay the bills. punch the clock. plow the fields. punch the clock. buy the stuff. always the stuff. punch the clock. put on the weight and punch the clock. hate yourself a little more each day. punch the house. fix the house. eat your hate. punch the kids. kiss the kids. eat the house and punch. 30 slaps like an open hand and the only thing worth thinking about is death. we're all a little syl some days.

still standing

coming off the 40 and something gets hold of me. i take a hard left at the corner where a schoolmate pulled out in front of a semi truck at 16 and was never heard from again. the tree that made the fatal blind spot still stands to this day and i find that strange. so i plod along down that road and the old barn i damn near broke every bone in my body jumping out of as a kid is still standing. tilted like the leaning tower of pisa but still standing and i find that strange. the drug den apartments in the adjacent field that i lived in as a baby are still standing with a fresh coat of paint to keep up appearances but still standing. and i find that strange. all the things that get hold of me when i'm coming off the 40 are still standing and calling out to come around and visit. and i find that strange.

wondering about vertigo

since when did i have vertigo? and shouldn't sitting solve that? that strange feeling of sinking into the couch catches up with all of us at some point. i just didn't think it would be so soon. didn't think that toppling out of a park swing would ever be a thing. that i would have to take a second to think where i am while dusting down the bark chips and laughing the whole thing off. i wouldn't have dreamed of coming to gasping for breath like that day at the beach when high tides rolled seaweed over my body while the salty waves plugged my lungs. i feel that way all the time now. confused and plugged up by salty waves wondering where i am and when i got vertigo.

nothing to give

i got nothing. nothing to give. nothing to say. no courtesy to the 20 something popping bubble gum in the elevator next to me. no patience for the blower outside moving fall leaves in circles. let them rot like everything else and return to earth and dirt the way nature intended. that reminds me to make a note to call my attorney. make sure my will states clearly to cremate me. to plant a tree and put my ashes in the soil. give something back for everything i took. pay my debt ya know? so long as it's not today. today i've got nothing to give. the sound of popping gum and leaf blowers are stuck in my head.

never learned to settle

dust. hate the stuff. i see it in everything. couches. clothes and hair. people's faces and in their countenance. barking dogs and cell phone calls. produce isles and countertops. dust. sit. stand. sleep. dust. i can't escape it. i never learned to settle down the way dust does. to loaf and land wherever i please and just be. a particle without purpose. but i never learned to settle. i started rubbing early on and now i can't turn it off. always waxing. always wiping. always brushing. always brooming. i never learned to settle.

where they go we can't follow

i once was told that we go deep within ourselves just before death. and i've seen that on people waiting to die. there's a distance in their eyes that convinced me of it. i think them in a grand library of their lives thumbing through the pages of the best and worst of themselves. they whisper things at night between the silence and creaky floors. little phrases through rattling lungs. makes you wonder which book and what chapter they're in. makes you wish you had a manuscript to follow along. see what mischief they're up to. what drives a smile across their twitching cheeks. why they raise their hand to say something about that last sentence. people go deep within themselves that way just before death and it hurts to know that we can't follow along.

winter is a mood

winter's always cold for me. can't get warm enough. doesn't matter what i do. it's the feet i think. never enough circulation. causes conflict deep in the sinus cavity. the pressure that pushes to the back of my ears and puts me in a pissy mood. winter's a mood.

when the silly games are over

heads up seven up and i've got my eyes on the ground. i love to cheat like that. there was always a way to cheat at every game and i got my kicks from scowling peers. evened up the playing field in my favor. gave me something to take home and have to myself. ends don't justify the means sometimes but i never claimed to be a saint. cheating when you're older gets harder. there aren't any teachers around to force the other kids to keep playing and it gets lonely when you don't have anyone to play with. nothing to take home. to have to yourself when the silly games are over. heads up seven up and no one's tapping my shoulder.

about the time

i started swearing pretty early. mom always said she'd slap my mouth if she heard it. that's about the time i started lying. mom said she'd slap my mouth if she found out. that's about the time i learned how to run. mom said she'd slap my mouth if she caught me. that's about the time i learned to hide. mom said she'd slap my mouth if she found me. i started my bad habits pretty early. swearing. lying. running and hiding. mom said she'd slap my mouth but i'm still swearing. lying. running and hiding.

laughter over love

i'm writing you that night long before we were the people we'd become. the evening sky was northern lights and techno temperament. i never let you love me. i could have but i didn't. i chose to melt into the backseat and have a laugh instead. cigarette buzzed with vodka brain i chose to have a laugh instead.

life as a fish

summer heat makes me indolent. lazy the way fish get when the water warms up. life would be better as a fish. i dream that on summer days. thumbing my nose at pretty things trolling through the water. swimming upstream and spawning in river bottoms. living and dying for swimming upstream to spawn in river bottoms. i dream that on summer days. the heat makes me indolent and i am a fish.

tahoe snow

the tahoe snow might have done it. might have got us thinking too much about things. or maybe it was the cold. the kind between us in the air and in our hearts. maybe it was the sierra earthquakes. the ones that shook our bed and tempers. maybe it was the way the road leaned into the winding curves beneath the giant sugar pines. or maybe it was the quiet on the long road home. whatever it was we knew. we knew that tahoe was going to hurt. that tahoe was going to break our hearts. it's hard to think it could have been anything else. that maybe it was us. was me. was you. it's hard to think it could have been anything else so we put it on the tahoe snow.

god or something like it

western desert heartache is a real thing. the stories there are old as time. older. old as dirt and wind. you can't help but picture god or something like it wandering around out there all alone wondering what the point of this existence is. i think god wonders about that too. if man is made in god's image i think god wanders and worries just like we do. the responsibility of it would drive anyone to the western deserts to wander and wonder. questioning creation and asking yourself if you did too much or too little. will they get it? will they know the gift when the time is right or will they live as mad poets wandering and wondering in the western deserts? the heartache out here is real and you can't help but picture god or something like it wandering alone.

people go their way

let's keep the things we can't change out of it. i've tried. tried asking the ones i love to put the bottle down. to come back for the rest of us. i've held onto the pain in their eyes when they told me to mind my own business. i filed it down with the other things. nobody should have told me to do that. to put me in that position and use me to ask something they couldn't ask themselves. now i have to carry that for both of us. i had more room for it when i was younger but now i'm running out and i can't keep finding new space for old baggage. people go their own way and i don't have to be their storage unit. took me a long time to understand that. so let's keep the things we can't change out of it. i've tried.

moonlit blacktops

we never wondered about the clouds and sun back then. the golden hills above tehachapi had other plans. we got busy hunting tarantulas in the midday heat and running off raccoons at midnight. sneaking out of that tiny 3 bedroom and walking the moonlit blacktop of golden hills was the rush of our little lives but we never wondered about the clouds and sun or what they saw and knew. we were too busy being boys on the run from childhood and simple things and chasing our adult selves down the moonlit blacktop of golden hills. eventually we caught up and waved those boys goodbye and now some part of me wants to go back that way and park out front of that tiny 3 bedroom to see if i can't catch those boys sneaking out to walk that moonlit blacktop. because i do wonder about the clouds and sun these days. high above the golden hills of tehachapi. would they know me? know my heart and regret in chasing? know that i'm tired? tired of running after myself and chasing a younger me down moonlit blacktops?

spirits of buried thoughts

november has a special kind of cold that burrows deep into my skin. gets clear through to the bone some days and i can never get comfortable. soaking in a warm bath until i'm lobster red just irritates the skin but i can still feel the sting of frostbite carrying through my toes. they have a special way of keeping grudges. the toes. especially mine. some of my deepest shame is stored in my feet and november has a special kind of cold that burrows deep in my skin through to my bones where it calls out into cells of fogged memory cemeteries. the cold calls for the spirits of buried thoughts to rise up and remind me that i once very nearly killed my own father when he was changing brake pads on his car. the vehicle had shifted in place and slid from the stabilizing blocks falling directly on top of him. the full weight of it crushing him beneath. my uncle had screamed in vain at me inside the house. calling me to phone an ambulance. i tried desperately to work the numbers but i was confused amid the chaos. meanwhile my father slipped further from life. seizing and shaking to an untimely death. fortunately a neighbor nearby heard the commotion and was able to help with the phone call and get paramedics to our home. i'm still not sure how my father survived the incident but he did. a long thick welt stayed across his chest for weeks after that and november cold has a special way of calling to those spirits of buried thoughts to remind me.

i keep running

dead black flies in the stairwell on my run this morning. frozen solid but i keep running. outside my building there's only the birds and quiet. a man kicks open the door to my building with a gigantic foot. he is tall and very obese walking with a cigarette and texting on his phone. he doesn't look up to cross the road. i scream to the birds to flee from this place. back to the woods where they belong. the smoking pigs have taken over here and there is nothing for them. they scatter and chatter amongst themselves and i keep running.

life on the rio grande

a photo of two women and their children came into my feed today. the women are unkempt and heavy from carrying multiple children. each is adorned with tattoos and there's a distance in their eyes that suggests a dissonance that can only be brought on by uncertainty. their children play naked in the background on the muddy banks of the rio grande river. the caption below states that the women are both 28 respectively but their soft bodies and hardened faces would infer otherwise. i pause to reflect on the poignancy of the photo. the hardened faces of young women and their children on the rio grande river. a look of dissonance brought on by uncertainty.

death on an old mountain trail

a rattlesnake once took me by surprise on the peak of an old mountain trail. i pushed my sons back and immediately grabbed a nearby boulder and held it above me. in the next moment i would bring that rock down on the snake's head and end its time on this earth. the snake paid me no mind and slowly moved away from us oblivious to its imminent demise. there was a confidence in the way it moved and i lowered the boulder in admiration. the snake knew the face of death that day but endeavored to go on living on its own terms. i too have taken death by surprise and looked upon its face as it held a boulder over my head. i too have endeavored to live life on my own terms until i cross paths with death once more. perhaps a descendant of that snake will meet me out on that old mountain trail and escort me out of this plane of existence. i will know when that time comes and i will not hold the boulder.

the theory of time

the eyes of a person holding a loaded gun in your face can tell you everything you'll ever want to know. all the great mysteries of the universe are revealed in the space of a decision to pull the trigger or not. the first revelation in that space is that time is merely a human construct. it does not exist in this matrix. it is nothing more than a distraction man has given himself to discourage the seekers from asking the questions of the universe. the first humans knew the answers would prevent the next generations from making progress in their industrial evolution and that the final stage of humanity: the conclusion to our existence through convenience would not come to fruition without a mechanism to ensure the success of that final stage. thus the great machine was imagined and each new construct another cog or wheel in the apparatus. i have seen those truths in the eyes of a person holding a loaded gun to my face. they are passed down through the dna and live deep within us. there are small moments in life looking down the barrel of a loaded gun for instance when they are revealed to us. little openings in the matrix and we have only to look through to see them.

poetry is my penance

writing poetry hurts my feelings. i can't think of any other way to put it. the words are raw. naked as the drunk teens at high school parties i attended. running around the page with all the private parts hanging out for everyone to see. maybe i'll be embarrassed about that later when people laugh at the exposure. maybe i'll laugh a little at myself to ease my discomfort. maybe i'll remember why i wrote myself the bad guy and kept the rest of it buried. writing poetry hurts my feelings but i like it that way. because i have been the bad guy and poetry is my penance.

the sorrow of songbirds

read a line that made me weep today. something distressing about the sorrow of songbirds but i can't recall how it went. i'd meant to make a note of it but i never do the things i mean to and i never mean the things i do. it's a circle the way life is a circle. we don't mean to be born. to live a life and die a death. we don't mean to go on creating more lives that will do the same all in the name of keeping the circle going. putting out the trash on tuesdays. church and chicken dinners on sunday. folding the clothes and scrubbing the floors. cooking the dinners. rushing the littles to school. coveting coffee and offering subtle suggestions for christmas gifts. we don't mean to be greedy and self serving all in the name of keeping the circle going. just like i never mean to tailspin into a tangent because of a line i read that made me weep. we never do the things we mean to and never mean the things we do. we are the sorrow of songbirds and that is the line i'd meant to make a note of.

roads in small towns

roads in the small town i grew up in never change. the people there come and go. the houses weather and fade but the roads never change. trees wither and find their way back to the earth but the roads never change. i miss those bends and curves beneath my bicycle tire when i'm feeling lost. when i can't find direction in life. roads in the small town i grew up in never change and i need that sometimes. i need familiarity to get my bearings. to give me purpose again. when everything around me makes no sense i take comfort in the things that never change like roads in the small town where i grew up.

traditional americana

i no longer have a heart for traditional americana. a way of life thrust upon me as a child doesn't make sense to me anymore. it's a transformation thousands of years in the making and i've entered into the cocoon phase. i hope to emerge a butterfly soon of exquisite color and soar free far above the restraints of a life of confinement. from the watchful eyes of the mantis americana and its traditionalist claws. raptorial ligaments that would see fit to crush my spine whole. slowly consuming my vibrant colors. from that i hope to soar far and away from.

biding my time

i'm biding my time. holding out for the sun to burn up the last of its energy and fade away. i can't see any other recourse for humanity. we're a curious mistake of mud and molecules that rose up from the swell of oceans and found its way to the top of the food chain. our one great delusion was to think ourselves the sovereignty over all things when we are but lowly subjects of the one true deity at the center of our corner of the universe. it too must adhere to its master in time and so i'm biding mine. i see no other recourse for humanity. all things are without purpose.

the issue of being literal

could be that i read into things too much. but i always took the bible for its words. i learned to celebrate cynicism and to rejoice a father who demanded we love each other unless specified otherwise. to praise rage and tantrums in anger of choices made from free agency and to practice understanding in the plight of men who wage war and genocide in the name of. i've been called close minded when i could no longer subscribe to those notions. a simpleton who doesn't see the bigger picture. perhaps i am too literal. perhaps i do read into things too much. if only there were some conclusive doctrine to show me the way. something i could reference for clarity when my moral compass is off course. something transparent that i couldn't read into too much.

we're still wolves

i've heard them before. wolves in the woods at night. the way they howl at the midnight moon made my blood run cold. i didn't run away when they spoke though. i needed to know what i was made of besides flesh on bone. needed to know my constitution. the woodland creatures stood around me in the darkness curious of my disposition. i could not see them but i could sense their consternation. i didn't mean to alarm them but i too would soon be a wolf. for i was alone in the woods at night seeking out my brothers. the earth of men polluted and bloated with material desire had run its course. we had forgotten ourselves and our place. we too were wolves once. dogs remember that but we've forgotten. forgotten how we'd shed our fur for cooked meat. the meat that changed our minds but not our makeup. we're still wolves in human clothing. so if you're reading this find yourself alone at night and seek out your brothers. the moon will always welcome us back.

flakes of poetry

every poem is a part of me. flakes of skin that hit the page and arrange themselves to tell a story. to paint a picture of who i am in words. i enjoy the dark strokes where there's pain in my paintbrush. the things i've said and done that i'm not proud of. little flakes of skin that hit the page to tell a story. poems that used to be a part of me.

the sky knows

seagulls are fighting for a spot on a street lamp as i pump gas this morning. the violent flapping of white and gray wings gets my attention and i pause to watch the spectacle. whenever one seagull lands on a particular post it stomps around childishly to assert its dominance. moments later another seagull swoops in with violent wings forcing the previous victor to flee the coveted spot and fly shamefully away. the new supreme leader now stomps about childishly asserting its dominance. from the ground below i look on with squinting brows. there's a correlation here but the gas pump sounds off and i wrap up what i'm doing. i look once more to the seagulls and note that there are no new contenders. the sky is beginning to sulk and threaten rain. driving away it hits me: the seagulls have been watching us closely and the sky knows it.

no surprises

i'm not surprised by anything anymore. i can say that without a second thought. i've seen it all now and i stand by that. i shake my head at the things i can't understand and there's the rub. there's no shock value left. no second looking at male celebrities wearing a dress to a public event to get attention. i'll shake my head at the desperation but i'm not surprised. i can't recall the last time i was put off by something. maybe the time my cousin broke both his arms during a seizure? that could be it but it's hard to say. could have been much sooner that i became desensitized. some of us are born that way maybe. stripped of sensation i mean. like everything that happened in our lives is just deja vu. a recycling of past life experiences. so we're just walking around annoyed with having to be alive. miserable because we know that death will only continue that recycling in the next version of ourselves so suicide is nothing more than a duality of taking pain from one plane and speeding up the process for the next person. there is no happy medium. and all this because i read a warning on a package of flour advising people not to eat the flour raw. no surprises left. just head shaking.

mansion fire eyes

the heat of it was overwhelming but we stood and watched anyway. the fiery blaze that took that park city mansion on prom night. the day had been a complete bust. snowmobiling with a group of kids we didn't care about. corsages and coordinated dancing. not a single thing i can look back on from that day that i enjoyed. the mansion fire though… and that look in your eyes… something sinister as you gazed at the flames. i recall now that you invited me in later at the end of the night even after you'd said you wouldn't. something about a boyfriend but i didn't go in. the day had been a bust and i was pouty. i've pouted my way out of one too many opportunities though so i hope you never felt bad about that. i saw you years later when we were older and married. you were with your kids and me with mine at a dinosaur museum. i knew you right away but i don't think you knew me. i was different but you weren't. i wanted to say something but i couldn't make it past your eyes. that park city fire was still there high as the walls of hell and blazing so i pouted my way out of talking to you after all those years. and i hope you never felt bad about that.

worried about the words

ash in dirt. someday that'll be me. i don't fear that part though. i've seen what comes next but i'm keeping that one for myself. i'm haunted by the wondering. the worrying about the words. did they make it? did they find the people who needed them? give them something to think about? to live for? to die over? poets can't help that part. the worrying about the words. i'm ready for ash in dirt though. there's peace in that. i worry about the words. will they speak them 100 years from now? 500? i don't suppose they will. i'm not going out like cobain. i've got too much to say and too little time to say it. somewhere i'm ash in dirt already. but where are the words i wonder? did they make it? probably not. i didn't go out like cobain.

thinking about an elk

came upon a cow elk once that had tripped downhill and snapped its neck on a tree. something about that still pokes at me. makes me wish i could have been there to see it. i could never understand how such a graceful animal could do that. even now i can't picture it in my mind. 500 pounds of muscle and unparalleled agility useless against one little misstep. i've been dreaming about that elk lately. i can see everything as it was that day that i came upon it. been thinking that maybe the elk didn't misstep after all. thinking that maybe life got the better of it. life with all of its hot trends and chasing perfection. newer. bigger. better. get it now before they sell out! always something in front of us and we're always chasing. i've been dreaming about that elk lately and wondering. thinking maybe life got the better of it. seeing myself against that tree. my neck bent back staring up at myself. i am the elk. i am life.

J

Acknowledgments

To my family, friends, and amazing followers, I must express eternal gratitude. Your tireless support lifts my spirits daily and continues to give me strength and inspiration in my endeavors and writing. I truly could not chase my dreams without your love. If my words have reached you in any way, please, kindly leave a review for this book. Your time and thoughts are important to me.

About the Author

A lover of words and the impact they create, Ty Gardner is a lifelong enthusiast of all forms of poetry and has written creatively from the time he was a child.

When he's not musing and waxing poetic, Ty can be found exploring the wonderment of his newfound home in Northwest Arkansas with his wife, two children, and their handsome rescue pup, Archer.

He is the author of *By Way of Words: A Micro Prose Journey Through the Elements That Mold Us*, *Bukowski Charm: Trash Fire Poetry to Warm the Soul*, *From the Watercolor Garden: Poems of Life and Love*, *A Thousand Little Things: One-line Poems to Spark a Thought*, *Exercises in the Abstract: Poems With No Name*, *Sunsets Over Cityscapes: Poems for the Existential Uprising*, *Papercut: A Chap-style Book of Prose*, and *Average American: Poems On Becoming Normal.* Some of his works can also be found in *VSS365 Anthology: Volume One*, released in September 2019.

Printed in Great Britain
by Amazon

37809094R00066